THE **SEVEN STEPS** TO **PERSONAL** AND **PROFESSIONAL FREEDOM**

THE SEVEN STEPS TO PERSONAL AND PROFESSIONAL FREEDOM

How to Add Meaning to Your Ambition

JENNIFER BROADLEY

authorHOUSE®

AuthorHouse™
1663 Liberty Drive
Bloomington, IN 47403
www.authorhouse.com
Phone: 1-800-839-8640

Published by AuthorHouse   07/24/2012

ISBN: 978-1-4685-8343-4 (sc)
ISBN: 978-1-4685-8344-1 (e)

This book is printed on acid-free paper.

To Lydia who inspires me every day.
And to my amazing Mum and Dad—thank you.

Contents

Introduction:
Choosing Freedom Takes Know-How

> "For tomorrow belongs to the people
> who prepare for it today."
> **AFRICAN PROVERB**

Never before in the history of our planet has awareness and abundance been available to so many, so quickly and so simply. In perhaps just decades into the future, people will look back at this time and say, 'That's when the shift went stellar; that's when human momentum really took off; that's when mankind embraced a raising of consciousness never before available to the masses.'

It's from this point onward that individuals will contribute to the greater good on a scale that will alter their own lives and, by extension, their families, communities and nations.

These are exciting times, and you—yes *you*—have choices to make. Are you stepping up to design your personal and professional freedom? Are you ready for the shift from ambition to meaning. And are you ready to integrate abundance and fulfilment into your everyday life?

I've called the seven principles I detail in this book 'steps' because walking forward is one of the easiest things we do each day—and the hallmark of all inspired principles is simplicity. Knowing and applying the seven steps to personal and professional freedom will profoundly change your life.

> 'I found it so easy to think differently as a result of applying The 7 Steps,' said Deborah, the owner of a successful food-processing business from Cornwall, UK. 'And interestingly, I wanted to use them to work out a "post-work" scenario, but the reality is I've seen myself as still having something more to contribute to the entrepreneurial world I inhabit.'

> Deborah goes on to confirm that these are grounded personal and professional principles. 'What is good is I've seen myself changing the core of my approach from ambition to meaning, but the outer commercial shell remains. It's almost as though the bits of me that I like and that have meaning have been given permission to develop a commercial reality.'

What You Believe: Selecting Your Information

We live on a planet where most people are mostly good most of the time, yet we're surrounded by a global media industry that selects the most extreme examples of mankind's shadow side, promoting it as if it's a norm. It's time to question the validity of the information that's forming your beliefs and to take stock of what you think and believe as a result.

Most of us build up our information over months, years and decades, from a range of sources including family, friends, peers, colleagues, preachers, professors, newspaper and magazine articles, radio and tv shows, books, and acclaimed bloggers. None of it is absolute and all of it is debatable (depending on the freedom of speech laws which you allow yourself). Ultimately, when you take in all this information, your job is to develop a sense of what's valuable for where you're heading and what isn't—a sort of 'keep it in; chuck it out' process.

Regardless of the credibility of the source, some information will be irrelevant to you and the purpose you've chosen to live out. What applies to your mum, your best friend, or your fellow board members may not apply to you. There are as many 'right' ways as there are people choosing directions. In order to make those smart decisions about what information is valuable or worthless to you, you must know the answer to *one* essential question: What do you want?

Knowing the answer to this question is your first step to being able to make decisions that take you step-by-step towards the vision you're holding. Achieving abundance in *all* areas of your life is much more about what you let go of than what it is you learn. The limiting beliefs you grew up with are like ballast bags tied to a hot air balloon: they keep you down, low to the ground. Some of these common beliefs are as follows.

- A profession is best—choose *one* job and stick to it until you retire. It's dangerous to change career, especially when you have responsibilities.
- The bigger the company, the safer your job.
- You don't have to love your work—just be grateful you're paying your bills.

- A good relationship should last forever; if it ends, you've failed.
- There's one right faith, and if you don't believe what we believe, you're wrong.
- You can't be rich and also be enlightened.
- You'll never run that 10K race; none of your family was ever sporty.

Freedom comes from spotting your limiting beliefs and reassessing them, knowing what you know now about your infinite potential and what you want to see yourself realising in your lifetime. Most beliefs can go in the 'chuck it out' pile, leaving space for new, uplifting thoughts that confirm to you your ability to create a work-life legacy which amazes you.

About ten years ago in London, I had the pleasure of answering the door to a lovely woman who had come to tell me 'the good news'. I listened attentively and was in agreement until the bit about being 'saved from the darkness and violence of mankind'. First, that didn't sound like very 'good news' to me, and second, when weighed up against the experiences I'd accrued over four decades of international living, I decided that this information (though not all of it) was heading for my 'chuck it out' file.

When she finished, I explained, 'I agree that we're all part of one universal energy that is positive, uplifting, inspiring and loving. But then there's a huge gap between your 'being saved from evil' theory and my real life experiences. You see, my friends and family and I, occasionally have blips where we might get angry, speak insensitively, or even hit out, but those instances are super-rare. Mostly I meet good people, have uplifting and encouraging conversations and experience honesty and openness regularly.

'People are nice to me in shops and kind to my daughter in her buggy on the bus. I live in the most diverse city in the world—rich, poor, black, white, men, women, gay, straight, concrete skyscrapers and green parkland. Every day people are on the whole civil, polite and respectful. My true and biggest experience is that goodness is the predominant factor displayed by mankind.'

We debated some more and each of us left more enriched by the encounter.

As you read through this book, give some further thought to the 'facts' that may have existed in previous generations but are 'choices' in today's world; to 'opinions' held by leaders that may 100% apply to their purpose, yet only 5% apply to yours; and to 'beliefs' that served you healthily last year, but for these next twelve months you'd be smart if you reviewed them.

"A wise man changes his mind; a fool never will."
SPANISH PROVERB

The Essence of Quantum Physics—*Everything* Is Energy

Science and philosophy are in agreement on this fact: there is one energy pulsing through all things. It courses through the cells of everything that has physical form—you, me, buildings, buses, mountains, oceans and stars. It exists in the non-physical, too—your thoughts, feelings and intuition. And it continues to flow through the seemingly abstract—time, space, past and future.

This source energy (also known as the universe, higher intelligence, God, higher self—whatever is your experience of all that is) is in everything and is expressed in infinite ways, yet it is one overall entity. You yourself are part of that infiniteness, unique yet part of the whole at the same time.

Snatam Kaur, the American singer-songwriter, says in one of her lyrics:

> The sun shines on everyone . . . it doesn't make choices;
> The rain falls on everyone . . . it doesn't make choices;
> One spirit flows through everyone . . . it doesn't make choices.

You are not separate from other people, you are not separate from the things you want, and you are not separate from source energy. Think of yourself as being one drop in a vast ocean: the drop is in the ocean . . . *and* the ocean is in the drop.

I'm outlining this science side at the moment because it's important that, when you go on to read about the seven steps to personal and professional freedom, you understand this knowledge has been around for millennia and is credible, tested and proven.

As with all areas of knowledge, since its inception quantum physics has historically been understood and developed by an expert elite—physicists, philosophers, scientists and the wealthy and learned. However, the increased mass education of our children over the past two hundred years, combined with the last two decades' opportunity of globally sharing information over the web, has profoundly changed all of that.

The value of knowing the full implications of these three simple words, 'everything is energy', is really only in its genesis. Expert meta-physicians and soul-science practitioners have taught and continue to teach what they know. Their students are in turn testing and evolving that knowledge, and teaching their information to a wider tribe of eager truth-seekers and way-showers. But don't be fooled—these people are *not* sandal-wearing, dawn-chanting, guru types; they're business leaders, corporate innovators, professionals, parents, coaches, sportsmen and budding rock stars—people just like you!

In the next ten years we'll see a new generation of what the Buddhist faith refers to as *bodhisattvas*. This name refers to people living on purpose, anyone who is motivated by compassion and seeking enlightenment not only for himself or herself but also for the good of everyone.

> *In reference to The 7 Steps program, Pam, a housing professional from London, said, 'This has had a real impact on my life and the way that I think about and treat myself and others in my life. I now have a truly meaningful relationship with my daughter, a more open relationship with my partner, and a new, confident and brave approach to life. I'm so excited about the future.'*

Historically, human development has evolved like this:

- From the beginnings of civilisation, respect was given to those who understood the workings of the **body** and could heal others physically when necessary; medicine, nutrition, fitness and health have all improved over time.

- Then we've had centuries of formal and structured education—valuing the **mind**, developing the intellect and the power to reason.

- Now, with awareness around two human elements, there existed the potential of developing each to their maximum *and* the phenomenon of those two parts collaborating for increased possibility. A fit body has a positive effect on the mind and vice versa.

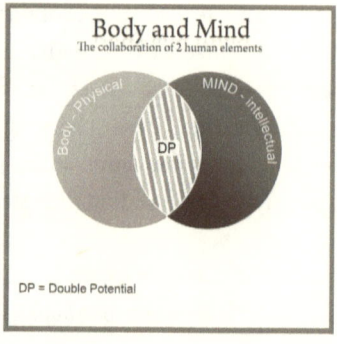

- In our very recent history (over the past hundred years), there has been a growth in understanding psychology and emotional intelligence—matters of the **heart**—and the healing and development of a person through an awareness of how he or she feels in response to specific circumstances.

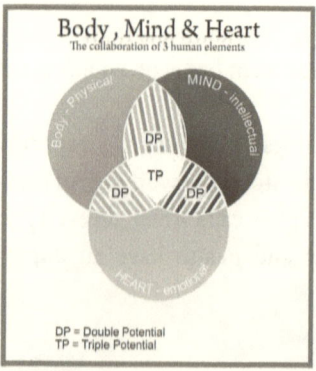

The diagram shows then that when you have awareness around three human elements, you have not one but three areas where you can experience double potential, and you create the possibility that when body, mind and heart are simultaneously active and healthy, there's now triple potential at your core.

- The final part of the puzzle has been last to develop because it's somewhat mysterious. It's the hardest to prove—and we know how important evidence is to credibility. The study of it is touched on in metaphysics, quantum physics, theology, philosophy and faith. I'm just going to call the combination of all of those disciplines 'soul science'.

Only with the knowledge of how your **soul** integrates with body, mind and heart can you consciously develop to where limited beliefs are transformed into infinite possibilities.

You'll see from this next diagram that with the collaboration of the soul into your life, there are multiple opportunities to reach double potential, as well as triple potential.

Success with Soul©
The collaboration of the 4 human elements

DP = Double Potential
TP = Triple Potential
QP = Quadruple (or Quantum) Potential

The remarkable part of this model though, is the existence of the fourth dimension, where you've quadrupled the possibilities.

The collaboration of all four human elements is

mankind's gateway to human capabilities en mass, giving rise to a new age of possibilities.

Your Soul and How It Works (The Simple Version)

Source energy (the intelligent power that exists in the physical and non-physical realms) is not a random flow of atoms and molecules. It has purpose and an intention for the growth and expansion of all things. In accessing source energy, you access the opportunity to know your unique purpose and to reveal over time the biggest expression of who you really are.

Using your soul to connect to source energy is like taking the plug of a toaster and connecting it with the electrical supply waiting in the power socket. Plugging in is the only way an appliance can come into its own, to fulfil what it was designed to do. The plug gives it access to an ever-present power; it's what gets a toaster toasting, a hair dryer drying and an audio system pumping out your music.

There's an expanding range of electrical appliances available to us, each designed to increase the ease of our life and none fulfilling their purpose until they're plugged in.

Similarly, there's an expanding range of people or souls coming into the physical world. Some are plugged into source energy from inception, some plug in seconds before they pass over and others access it somewhere in between.

Each soul has a very specific reason for choosing its time, parents, family, community and life experience. We are all connected, all intentional and all here for the playing out of something so vast and fantastical that the only response to our part in the plan must be to trust; some might call that response faith.

> *Chris, a senior media professional in the UK, said, 'Learning about The 7 Steps has been like a ray of sunshine. I've rediscovered self-belief in a manner which is entirely unrelated to ego and entirely related to my purpose. I'm daring to dream again and not worrying about the how.'*

Einstein said, 'The most important question you will ever have to answer is, "Is the universe friendly or is it hostile?"' He acknowledged an intelligent energy that flowed through particles, time and space, and he looked for proof from the world around him to evidence its character.

As many other experts before and since have concluded, the universe *is* love. It has a massive bias towards compassion, goodness, light, creativity and the expansion of individuals, communities and global consciousness.

What I've spent the last decade exploring is how each of us, in our own unique way, connect with this source energy. Where do we learn about our soul? What language is used to explain it to us (if it was ever explained at all)? And how effective has that actually been in creating the life we presently live and the choices we're making?

Here's the thing: if Einstein was right about this universal intelligence being kind, creative, and expanding (and there's evidence he's smarter than your average genius physicist), wouldn't it be of benefit to have a clear, practical, personal process to access what he was pointing to—the love, abundance and success available to me and you in every moment of every day?

My research over the past decade has lead me to listen to and learn from world experts, leaders, gurus, philosophers, preachers, teachers, masters, thinkers, industrialists, socialists, writers and broadcasters. I've distilled from them, and from connecting to source energy itself, an overarching set of principles that their collective theories and philosophies consistently acknowledge and point towards. These principles, which make up this book you're now reading, are simple and effective in their application. Just knowing about them, you can immediately up-level your thinking and results. You can be more, do more, have more and contribute more towards the expansion of your successes in all areas of your life.

In developing yourself in a soul-conscious way, you'll learn to love and accept yourself; in doing this, you increase your ability to love and accept others. It's the most important activity you can invest in: connecting soul to source and aligning yourself with your true purpose. It's the reason for you being. It's your highest calling.

Ask yourself what would perfect look like for your life. Physically, intellectually, emotionally and spiritually, what would be your best and highest self? Take a few minutes right now to consider that question—maybe even to write something down. Ultimately these are the questions that form your vision. If your picture isn't magnificent, inspiring, and totally unique to you, then you've got some bigger thinking to do.

So what are the seven steps that are going to shift you from where you are now to living out the vision your soul came forth to experience and which you've been holding in your heart since, well, forever? We'll look at each step in detail over the coming chapters. In short though, there are seven overarching principles that apply in all great examples of human achievement, whether by individuals, leaders, organisations, cultures or faith groups. They're powerful strategies, and although changes can occur immediately, you become conscious of what you're creating moment to moment and mastery of the principles can take a lifetime.

In defining these seven steps, my intention is to provide you with a choice: either take action now and use the steps to fast-track your personal and professional freedom, or take it all in and just ponder and review the information for a while. Whatever your own timing is, remember that while the destination counts, it's the way in which we journey that show the hallmarks of self mastery.

"True nobility is not about being superior to another.
True nobility lies in being superior to your previous self."
HINDU PROVERB

STEP 1
Clear and Courageous Thinking

"Simplicity, clarity, singleness: These are the attributes
that give our lives power, vividness and joy as they are
also the marks of great art. They seem to be the
purpose of God for his whole creation."
RICHARD HOLLOWAY

In this chapter you'll learn that even the non-physical has
energy. Most significantly this applies to your thoughts,
which create a reality for you every minute of every day;
your subconscious takes up the job at night time. Cultivating
the health of your thoughts is a skill set and takes time and
discipline. The rewards exist in every moment and rarely as
you expect them.

In a context of 'everything is energy', the most important
principle to know and master is that *thoughts become things*.
When you think happy thoughts, you attract happiness; when
you think anxious thoughts, you experience stress. When you fill
your head with thoughts about successful business, you filter in
the information that increases the likelihood of creating exactly
that.

Since what you think about comes to be, then it's of the utmost importance that you get clear and courageous.

- **Clear**—If anyone in the world has to know what you want for your life, it's you. There's immense power in knowing what you want to experience in your work, your health and fitness, your relationships, your friendships and your precious free time.

  Clarity increases the number of thoughts you have on a specific, desired outcome—like focussing a laser. Instead of thinking generally that 'a bigger house would be nice someday', your thoughts become specific: 'I love that in my five-bedroom, sea-view barn conversion, I can have my friends to supper, and I can chat with them from my open-plan kitchen while they all catch up with each other about their week. There's loads of space to chill out with games, movies and conversation well into the early hours.'

- **Courageous**—The most frequent factor that hinders people from fulfilling their potential is their inability to *boldly* dream their dream. If your thoughts are founded on scarcity, fear and poverty instead of abundance, courage and infinite possibilities, then how is your skyscraper going to get built?

  It's empowering to thing big, and more for you doesn't mean less for someone else—that's not how the universe is designed. Stretching yourself to explore the most courageous outcomes raises your energy to a level where infinite possibilities and quantum leaps become real.

If you take only one thing from this book take this: Thoughts become things.

> *Catherine, a mother and visionary and one of my executive coaching clients from London, said about this first step, 'I was absolutely stuck at the "clear and courageous thinking" stage. My second session, though, was like acupuncture for the soul, unblocking and releasing like crazy. I let go of barriers that I'd created with the best of intentions but which didn't serve my purpose anymore. It was a huge breakthrough for me, along with the realisation that the vision comes first, not the how.'*

Have you ever noticed that when people achieve to a world-class level, they're often labelled lucky or are described as being in the right place at the right time? But it's often the same achievers who 'luckily' thought harder about their success than anyone else in their field. And as 'luck' would have it, they spotted opportunities that others missed and then invested months, years and even decades in perfecting their skill set—whether it be tennis, cookery or business. Yep, 'lucky' Serena Williams, Delia Smith and Sir Richard Branson!

I once watched a TV chat show that had David Beckham, the world-class footballer, as one of the guests. The host asked David, 'What do you think contributed to you becoming the footballer sensation that you are today?'

David answered, 'I dreamed about it ever since I can remember.'

Another guest turned to him and said, 'Well, that's not an answer; every little boy dreams about being a legendary footballer. Even I dreamed that dream.'

David Beckham replied, 'Well, I dreamed it harder.'

His results show that probably he did dream it harder. This is one of millions of examples which show that whether you're aware of it or not, you're continually creating your own reality, thought by thought, conscious and subconscious, every second of every day.

Have you ever heard an actor say during an interview, 'I've pictured myself being on the big screen since before I could talk. I made up songs in my room as a child, my friends and I created imaginary plays and performed them to our families as an audience, and I persuaded my parents to pay for singing and acting and dancing lessons. It's all I thought about, all I spent my time doing'?

And how many autobiographies have you read where a billionaire entrepreneur will say something like, 'I remember at six years old, my uncle who worked in a sweetie factory and he used to come round for tea and bring boxes of toffees for us all to share. I used to take my handful of them, take them to school the next day, and sell them at five pence each to the kids in the playground. Trading and making money has fascinated me for decades. It's all I remember thinking about. It made me feel alive'?

Throughout history, millions of people have *thought* their way into the reality of a successful life. They've seen themselves in that penthouse overlooking Monte Carlo harbour; swimming with sharks and televising it for the world to see; they've run orphanages serving millions of street children; or they've presided over a country to lead it towards new industry, growth and a higher quality of life for all. In most cases these realities were being created decades before they fully manifested, and without conscious knowledge of this powerful first step of clear and courageous thinking.

Using a tool as simple as this is powerful because it offers freedom to observe your present life situation and to evolve your thoughts to create a similar or a completely contrasting future.

Even in the dampest, inner-city flat, surrounded by cold, unemployment and addiction, the skill of building up your thought muscle can begin. When you start to notice how the thoughts that you think influence the experiences you attract, you've tapped into a strategy of which few in history have been aware and that fewer still have mastered.

As you practice shifting your attention towards better feeling thoughts, your reality will adjust. I've see people consciously shift their thinking and then see results in minutes or days. I've also seen results happen on many levels. I remember one client deciding that he would hold the thoughts of his next pay review delivering a ten-thousand-pound increase, only to call me later *that same day* to tell me that an impromptu meeting with his director had delivered an unexpected bonus of ten thousand in recognition of his work during the last six months.

As you adjust your thoughts, you can expect to see small changes begin to occur. It might be that a friend rings your doorbell and suggests a coffee together. A letter from an aunt with a large cheque enclosed could appear through the mail. You're cooking supper and choosing 'power thoughts' when a favourite song comes on the radio and inspires you to get up and sing into your wooden spoon.

The positive effect of choosing better feeling thoughts is infinite. The power for a fulfilled future is 100 per cent within your control.

The Main Points

- **Everything is energy**
- **Thoughts become things**
- **Clear and courageous thinking positions you for infinite possibilities**
- **The thoughts you think today are creating tomorrow's reality**
- **Mastering your thoughts takes discipline; the rewards appear as part of the practice, though, not only at the point of ultimate mastery**

How to Take the Clear and Courageous Thinking Step

1. **Define Your Vision and Write It Down**
   Take a new page in a new notebook you're going to use for this purpose to document the extraordinary journey that starts right now. In the first page, define the following:

   - When am I at my happiest?
   - What are the elements of my most fulfilling lifestyle?

   You can think through some or all of these categories if it's helpful for you.

 o Relationships

 o Work/career

 o Family and friends

 o Finances & multiple income sources

 o Fitness and health

 o Personal development & new learning

 o Free time activities

 o Contribution to the greater good

Remember, you're not defining what you think is possible for you in the future; you're creating clarity around your ultimate vision. Be clear and be courageous—that is, don't compromise. At this stage you don't have to know the how of you getting what you want; rather you just have to dream big.

2. Create a Vision Board

In case writing isn't your thing, you can create a vision board. A vision board is a large piece of white or coloured paper which you cover with pictures, sketches and words that inspire you. Cut words, headings, and photos out of magazines, print images off the internet and draw what you see in your mind's eye. Glue all the pieces together on your board (or as pages in a notebook). The key is to look at the vision board every day and imagine yourself in the situations you've defined.

The idea in both the writing and the visualising is that the more you fill your head with pictures, thoughts, words and reminders of what you want to attract, the more convincing it is to your subconscious, the less resistance it puts up to keep things the same and the faster you're going to see results.

3. **Commit to a Five-minute Quiet Time, Morning and Night**
    This is a small investment to make in order to accelerate
    the manifesting of your vision. In these quiet times, choose
    a place where you won't be disturbed, close your eyes and
    for about one minute focus on your breathing. Begin to
    consciously breathe deeper and slower.

    Bring to your mind each element of your vision: surroundings,
    how you feel being there, what you hear, what you smell, who
    you are with. Fill in as many details as possible—it's *your*
    dream, after all—put yourself in the centre of the vision, and
    notice how what you're thinking impacts how you feel.

    This quiet-time activity is the spiritual equivalent of doing
    fifty sit-ups morning and night above and beyond your
    daily activities. It's a conscious time of plugging in to source
    energy and it creates a foundation from which the rest of
    your awareness can grow.

Feel It to Reveal It

"There can be no knowledge without emotion. We may
be aware of a truth, yet until we have felt its force,
it is not ours. To the cognition of the brain must
be added the experience of the soul."
ARNOLD BENNETT

**This chapter explores how the thoughts you're choosing
express themselves in every cell of your body. That
expression emits a resonance out into the wider world; you
attract back experiences on that same resonance. The less
you judge or limit those experiences, the more potentially
creative the outcome.**

We live in a vibrational universe. Every cell of every thing with
form is vibrating at a specific resonance, and that resonance is
open to adjustments with every thought you choose. It's like
turning the dial of a radio and letting each station amplify its sound
out through large, pulsating speakers. Personal and professional
freedom is created through what you're attracting into your
life each day—people, circumstances, opportunities, learning
experiences, mentors, clients, money, health and happiness.

Think about a time in your past when, for a full day, everything was perfect and you felt great: perhaps you were with friends, or walking hand-in-hand through an outdoor food market in France, or walking by the sea with your dog. Whatever it was, take a moment to absolutely picture yourself there, loving and enjoying what you see and hear, what you're touching, tasting and sensing. Does it feel good?

Now, take a moment to recall your first day at high school or at a new job. Think about not knowing where everything is. 'Who are all these new people? Will I fit in? Do I have to spend the next five years of my life here? I don't know my time table or who to ask for when I'm stuck. I don't know how to use this computer system . . .' That feels less good, right?

It's important that you begin to develop a full awareness of the spectrum of what you're feeling—and most importantly, the thoughts you were thinking just prior to that feeling becoming present.

People do not, as commonly assumed, think things because they feel them ('I don't know why I thought that; I guess it's just how I feel'). The thought always comes first. Admittedly it can be tricky to spot the thought if it's been offered up by your subconscious (a whole other area of study), but with practice and awareness you'll soon be able to spot and manage even those.

Energy organises around what is most articulate in your system. It's important to equip yourself with a colourful vocabulary around the subject you're passionate about. Practice *speaking out* how great it's going to be to achieve that promotion, drive that car, date that guy, build that house and have six-pack abs. Everything is achieved with less effort when our predominant vibration is one of already having achieved the result of which we're dreaming. When our predominant resonance is one of peace, we attract peace; when it's one of confusion, we attract mixed messages; when it's one of compassion, we attract love. This step places the success of your life squarely in the realm of your own self-development and your management of your emotions.

To understand this principle fully, it's helpful to look to quantum physics. It's common knowledge that at the core of each of the ten trillion cells which make up our human bodies, there's a swirling mass of energy. That energy can vibrate at an infinite number of frequencies and is predominantly controlled by our subconscious until we actively choose to manage the results ourselves. It's the subsequent resonance or emitting vibration that becomes what people sense about us.

You attract to you all things that vibrate on a similar frequency. You might have heard the saying, 'Like attracts like.' Well, 'Feel it to reveal it' is what that's all about. When what you *feel* with your heart and soul—your energetic self—matches what you want in your life, you'll sense a flow, a 'rightness', a relief about it. With that comes an ease in attracting those things that you want into your day-to-day experiences: love, money, fitness, choice, business and career opportunities.

Some call this the Law of Attraction. In the spirit of simplicity, here's how it works.

- Think it
- Believe it
- Feel it
- Receive it

In a job I held in my twenties, I worked for an international magazine company, managing the circulation of their titles in the UK and overseas. I'd been there for about three years and needed to meet with the human resources director to talk about a change I wanted to make. I rarely saw this woman about the building, and I wanted to keep the meeting as informal and non-official as possible. I didn't want to book an official time with her—I thought it would be better if I just bumped into her.

So, one night I started to picture what the perfect scenario would look like. I imagined myself going into work early, getting into the lift, and then this HR director would arrive seconds later and get into the lift with me; it would be just the two of us. I'd turn to her and say, 'Good morning, Marcia. I'm glad I bumped into you. I'd love to come and talk to you sometime today, if you have a spare twenty minutes.' She'd smile and say okay.

I thought it and felt it, and *the very next morning,* that exact scenario played out just as I'd imagined in my meditation!

I didn't know about the Law of Attraction in my twenties, but I now know that regardless of our starting point in life, everyone has equal access to this and every universal principle—that's why they're universal. You're using them daily, subconsciously and without having full awareness of the power and freedom available to you.

I once was in a huge rush to finish a half day at work and get my daughter to a lunchtime play date that had been arranged with the daughter of a woman I didn't know very well. I wanted to take a bunch of flowers with me and knew there was no time to get down to the flower stall and make it to this appointment. In my rush, I called on the Law of Attraction. I stopped just before stepping out of my front door, calmed down, and imagined the scenario of the universe taking care of the flowers and of my anxiety. I felt further relaxed and then stepped out with my daughter into the street to get in the car. That whole process took about twenty seconds.

As I was opening my car door, I heard someone call my name. 'Oh, I'm so glad I caught you before you went out! I wanted to give you these.' Here was my neighbour's brother, visiting from France for just two days, handing me a bunch of flowers just to say a thank-you for a small, random favour I'd done him a month beforehand. Wow! Just like that. Sorted.

Were these things a coincidence? Would they have happened if I hadn't taken a moment to picture what I'd wanted and shift my resonance from stress to trust? All I know is that in my work, teaching the practical application of these seven steps, I have the privilege of hearing stories like this every day.

Another small but essential point: Perhaps you read that flower story above and came away from it thinking, 'How ungrateful she was. Those flowers were for her, and she gave them away. It would have been better if she went to the flower stall, and it turned out she got them for nothing.' However, the universe has an infinite number of ways to fulfil your desires and requests. The less you define the how, the more scope source energy has to deliver the unexpected in an instant.

My coaching clients regularly manifest apparently random successes—things like key business meetings, phone calls offering new and perfect jobs, a gift of a car, salary increases in the exact amount envisioned, bumping into a woman at a library who eventually becomes a life partner, a meeting on a train that evolves into a six-figure business opportunity. There are so many stunning examples of holding a clear intention and letting the how be taken care of by the universe.

The Main Points

- **The thoughts you pick influence the resonance you emit**
- **You attract experiences that match your resonance**
- **Think it; believe it; feel it; receive it**
- **Let go of the how and let source energy present the unexpected**

How to Take the 'Feel It to Reveal It' Step

1. Pay Attention to Your Emotional Shifts

Start to pay attention to what naturally gives you a lift or makes you feel inspired. Is it certain types of people, conversation, activities, music, sports, times of the day, food groups, movies or books? Get to know your positive triggers and consciously choose to use more of them.

The more you are clear of your power and your ability to attract into your life the things you are emotionally aligned with, the more directly (and often speedily) those things will begin to appear.

You've often heard the saying, 'I'll believe it when I see it.' Well, the truth is the exact opposite: *you'll see it when you believe it.* That is, you'll manifest what you resonate.

The *Oxford Dictionary* says belief is 'the feeling that something is real or true; trust, confidence'.

You see—the feeling! The things you learn prompt you to think certain thoughts, which become your beliefs, which define how you feel, which attract your life experiences. So if you want a different result, learn something new, think different thoughts ... and believe.

Be conscious of the 'coincidences' that start to happen: an unexpected phone call, a chance meeting, an article you read online, a cheque through the mail, an opportunity for leadership. Every experience, whether you accept it in that moment or choose to pass it up, is something you've attracted to move yourself closer to your dream and your unique purpose.

Practice the habit of noticing your feelings shift from moment to moment, and of asking yourself, 'How is this resonance drawing me closer to my purpose?' Think consciously and feel passionately.

2. **Consciously Choose Better Feeling Thoughts**
   Here is where the first and second steps combine to create some magic. Like regular exercise, the more you invest time in picking positive, uplifting, affirming and inspired thoughts, the more fit and energised your thought muscle becomes. As a result, the more time you can spend contributing at your highest level.

   The first step to choosing better feeling thoughts is to become aware of the thoughts that have created your present reality—the thinking that's served to get you this far.

Then, when you're in that conscious state, notice how you're feeling and actively choose a series of better feeling thoughts, until you sense your resonance changing. When you're doing this effectively, you'll feel an instant sense of relief. It's the letting go of an old, limiting paradigm and your ten trillion body cells dropping the weight of that ballast.

Here are some examples.

Usual Thought	Better Feeling Thought
Not another spreadsheet.	I get faster at creating these and ultimately it's a skill I'll use when I run my own business. It's just a matter of time before the right opportunities present themselves. This is such a great time of preparation.
I'm crazy to believe I can afford a house like that.	It's not my job to know the how. I commit to seeing myself living the life of my dreams; I only need to know the next step and to take it. Keep it simple, keep trusting. There are millions of examples of ordinary people living extraordinary lives—that's my intention.
What if I say what I really think? People will think I'm nuts.	It's me who knows the details of my life and what I aspire to next. I only need my own approval. I'm good at what I do, and I'm an amazing, creative thinker. When I step up and speak out, I'm contributing ideas, products and services that can make a real difference. I'm so excited for what's coming up.

| I'll do whatever keeps him happy, whatever keeps the status quo, for the sake of the children. | I am infinitely resourced to get a better result from all situations. I choose to have only respectful and fulfilling relationships in my life. I will aim to be respectful and encouraging at all times. I trust that clarity, boldness and my choice to see everything as good will serve to deliver me the highest outcome in this situation and in all challenges that present themselves. |

3. **Your One-step Dial-up**

If you are like me and you like to see things on a scale, then here's an emotional scale that Esther and Jerry Hicks define in their book *Ask and It Is Given*.[1] It goes from the lowest vibrating emotional state (22) to the highest (1).

1. Joy/Knowledge/Empowerment/Freedom/Love/ Gratitude
2. Passion
3. Enthusiasm/Eagerness/Happiness
4. Positive Expectation/Belief
5. Optimism
6. Hopefulness
7. Contentment
8. Boredom
9. Pessimism
10. Frustration/Irritation/Impatience
11. Overwhelmment
12. Disappointment
13. Doubt
14. Worry

---

[1] Ester and Jerry Hicks, *Ask and It Is Given*: Hay House UK, 2008

15. Blame
16. Discouragement
17. Anger
18. Revenge
19. Hatred/Rage
20. Jealousy
21. Insecurity/Guilt/Unworthiness
22. Fear/Grief/Depression/Despair/Powerlessness

The success for choosing a better feeling thought comes from practicing knowing where you are on the scale (which can change throughout a day) and picking a new story that will shift you up one or two steps at a time.

If the jump's any bigger than a couple of steps at once, it's too much of a stretch for your mind to believe. Don't try to get from revenge to contentment, but perhaps start by giving yourself permission to feel anger. It's still a step up the scale, and what you're trying to observe in yourself is a feeling of relief as your new thoughts shift you to a higher vibration.

STEP 3
Absolute Personal Responsibility

"Let everyone sweep in front of his own door,
and the whole world will be clean."
JOHANN WOLFGANG VON GOETHE

This chapter is about the importance of owning your thoughts, actions, attractions and results. Responsibility liberates you, and there are opportunities to stride towards your freedom in every moment. When you commit to lifelong learning, you keep pace with the expansion of the universe; with that comes choice and reward.

Life doesn't happen to you—it happens *for* you. Each of us has the freedom to choose which information to retain and which to discard. Everyone's 'keep-or-chuck' editing process is as unique as a fingerprint. What you keep evolves into your ongoing (often subconscious) thinking. What you think about adjusts your resonance; what you resonate is what you attract.

Consciously or otherwise, you are the creator of your life experiences. This step to freedom places the power of how your life evolves entirely in your court and it has to be present in a success strategy because without it, the energy of blame, denial, resentment and limitation can keep us stuck . . . forever.

It's not uncommon to slip into 'I'm not responsible' mode—it's a massive Western cultural norm. You'll hear it often in various phrases.

- 'If my boss wasn't such a control freak, we'd have nailed that project months ago.'
- 'If our shareholders focussed on more than just their investment, we'd be able to make bolder and more creative decisions.'
- 'If my parents had taught me about finances and money management, I wouldn't be in so much debt right now.'
- 'If my professor wasn't so ancient and stuck in her ways, she'd have recognised that my 'C-' thesis was actually 'A+' cutting-edge thinking.'
- 'If my wife would lose some weight, she'd feel better about herself, and we wouldn't fight so much.'
- 'If my children would listen to me, I could help them more, and they'd be happier.'

Every time you blame, you miss the opportunity to learn the lesson the moment is gifting you. You shift into a lower energy and reduce your power to attract the results you truly want.

Taking 100 per cent responsibility is a key success trait practiced by leaders, innovators, free thinkers and game changers. When you do it well, you stay aware of your capabilities, of where you want to be over the course of your life and of how each decision you make leads you closer to achieving your entire vision in full.

To perform to your highest potential, you must take full responsibility for your thoughts, feelings and actions. Further still, you'll become habitual in acknowledging the value in your successes and your mistakes. Over time you'll naturally begin to:

- spend time in environments that inspire you
- eat healthily
- keep fit
- talk with respect
- be compassionate
- encourage those around you
- self motivate
- take lessons from the experts (and the beginners!)
- push the boundaries
- celebrate difference
- trust your intuition
- and always, *always* stride passionately in the direction of your dreams.

Being fully responsible doesn't mean that as a boss, you can't give constructive feedback to your team; or that as a parent, you can't reprimand your child for repeatedly drawing on the wall; or that as a partner, you can't negotiate some mutually better way of communicating in your relationship. It *does* mean that each of those conversations has to be shared in a way that creates a win-win situation for everyone involved. If you can't find a 'more for all' solution immediately, you're going to have to think longer and get more creative.

In terms of overall freedom, maintaining personal responsibility keeps your energy powerfully in the core of your physical self. From this place you can commit your full force to an increasing, upward cycle. When you blame, resent, or get angry, your energy pours out of you towards the person or situation on which you're focussing. For however long it takes for you to call that energy back (and that could be seconds—or it could be years!), you're living in a state of depletion.

You know the vision you're creating for yourself—your purpose, your career, your dream home, your ideal relationships, your health, your wealth, your contribution to the planet and what makes you happiest. So, go inside for your guidance. Follow your intuition and listen to the wisdom of your soul.

The Main Points

- **Life happens for you, not to you**
- **A commitment to lifelong learning is a commitment to personal growth**
- **Responsibility is liberating**
- **Tap into your unlimited creativity to find a 'more for all' solution**
- **Aligning your experiences with living your purpose is an 'inside job'**

How to Take the Absolute Personal Responsibility Step

1. **Give up Blaming**
   Instead of focussing on another person's short falls, or blaming an event over which you exercised no input, ask yourself these four questions.

- Why am I attracting this situation? (Because in understanding steps one and two, you know that all experiences are attracted to you from the thoughts you've been thinking and the feelings they generate.)
- What outcome do I want now?
- Will what I want create a win-win outcome for all involved?
- What more could I do to take 100 per cent responsibility for my contribution to this?

2. **Be Accountable**

At the end of a project, a meeting, a day, or an event, do a five-minute review. Keep a notebook with you so you have a record of how your responses change and your wisdom grows over time.

Here are three power questions to ask yourself.

- What did I do well?
- What could I have done better?
- What will I do differently next time?

This process is a commitment to your ongoing development, and it's a powerful and daily way to use every situation, conversation and event to deepen your learning of your own capabilities and to remain in a perpetual state of growth.

Take Inspired Action

"Everything you want is out there waiting for you to ask.
Everything you want also wants you. But you have
to take action to get it."
JULES RENARD

In this chapter you'll learn about your soul's agenda and how it uses your intuition to help you spot the next right move. You'll also see how the language of intuition is unique to you, which makes it important to know how it can prompt your attention, and how the rewards of taking action 'in spirit' can transform your life from greyscale to pantone.

Inspired action is when you make something happen knowing that it's part of your highest purpose or vision. It's about operating out of that core, quantum potential place. You can take action from a mindset of fear ('Any activity is better than no activity. I just need to be doing something') or from a mindset of trust ('Strange as this next step feels, I sense it's the right thing'). The difference between those two approaches is like navigating a five-hundred-mile road trip by jumping in the car, heading out in the general direction and working the rest out as you drive;

or by confirming the final destination and listening to the satnav instructions on the way.

Your route planner for living on purpose is your soul. It had an expected destination long before it entered the body that everyone now knows as you. However, your life is not predetermined. You can choose your journey—your jobs, the company you keep, the goals you set and your relationships. When you give yourself enough listening time, you'll hear your soul letting you know whether each choice you make is moving you closer to or further from that purposeful destination. Some situations and conversations will ignite your soul and add to your fulfilment, whilst others will leave you feeling disengaged and possibly in conflict with yourself or those around you.

To become masterful at taking inspired action, it's essential to learn to spot the promptings of the soul in any one moment. For most of us those triggers present themselves through our intuition, which is the ability to understand something instinctively, without the need for conscious reasoning. Intuition is not conscious, it's not from the mind.

> A director in a UK government agency said, 'Whilst practicing The 7 Steps, my ability to take inspired action was tested with a situation at work. A staff member made an off-the-cuff remark about her safety at work to a junior staff member. I immediately had a feeling that this was something that was deeper and was going to become a real issue. I cleared my diary for the afternoon and met the staff member. I then found out that she had been getting advice about her employee rights, and that she felt unsupported, although she had not escalated her concerns. I was able to put measures in place in the short

term and then in the longer term take legal action to ensure that her safety was not compromised.'

Your intuition can be a feeling in your core (your stomach area), on your skin, or around your heart area. It's different for different people, and it develops as we practice listening to it and taking action based on what we understand in the moment.

Have you ever noticed how little silence we factor into our daily lives? Distractions are everywhere and are on the increase. There's the radio on in the morning at breakfast, the iPod on the bus, back-to-back appointments at work, lunch with a colleague, the iPod on the way home, TV at the gym, the Internet in the evening, a few drinks and a bit more TV at home, and half a chapter of a book before your eyelids become so heavy you switch off the light and move swiftly into a deep sleep.

This persistent activity engages your conscious mind almost permanently. It also deafens you to the voice of your intuitive satnav—your soul—telling you how on or off course you are in living your purpose. You can block out your life design for only so much of your life, while your subconscious keeps you in the safe zone—the unexpanded version of the true you. In cases of extended denial, the cracks begin to show—overeating, under-eating, drinking, drugs, stress and anxiety, conflict situations, overworking, unfulfilled relationships and physical and mental illnesses.

Don't worry though, there's more hope and light on the planet today than ever before!

The word 'inspired' means 'outstanding or brilliant in a way or to a degree suggestive of divine inspiration'. Can you imagine living on purpose every day and taking actions prompted directly by source energy? You'd be presenting the very best of yourself to the world, fuelled by a burning desire that's in alignment with all of nature. That's *got* to be worth ten minutes of silence and contemplation each day. And that's all it takes to begin to recognise the character of your soul and to amplify your freedom to be truly and authentically you!

Inspired action is what drove the Wright brothers to fly the first airplane in 1903 despite much mockery; it's what motivated Emmeline Pankhurst to press on with her campaign of suffrage until all UK women were granted the right to vote in 1928; it's what kept Roger Bannister training until he broke the 'impossible' four-minute mile in1954.

I'm not saying that if you follow your purpose, your life will suddenly become carefree and easy. However, you will undoubtedly have an increased sense of ambition and desire, as well as a clarity about which actions will most effectively draw you into being part of the bigger picture. Engaging at the soul level will resource you in a wide range of ways for all your challenges. Without question, you living out your true passion will contribute to the world being a richer place for generations to come.

Inspired action—don't you just love that in partnership with source energy, every action you take is multiplied for good to a degree you can't possibly comprehend?

The Main Points

- **Acting 'in spirit' increases your results: do less, achieve more**

- **It's worthwhile becoming expert in the promptings of your soul**
- **Take action from a place of trust; face the fear and do it anyway**
- **In silence, your soul's purpose is amplified; listen in**
- **Every action you take is multiplied for the greater good**

How to Take the Inspired Action Step

1. **Learn to Interpret Your Intuition**
   What some people call intuition, others call soul or higher self. However you refer to it, it's the sense you feel in the core of your being that you're either off course or on track.

   Your intuition is the part of you that responds to divine intelligence, your connection to all that is. It's like a compass, always there for reference before you navigate your next move.

   Becoming conscious of your intuition means you have to tune in to the promptings of what you feel.

   - Trust your feelings, even if they don't make sense logically.
   - Act on them: say yes if they feel positive and on purpose; say no if you get the sense you'll be moving off track.
   - Bring yourself into the present moment as often as you can in a day. Remember your purpose, your vision and how far you've come. The very next action you take may be the one that brings you the breakthrough you've been waiting for.

2. Focus beyond the Action to the Outcome

Inspired thought can arrive in your mind with varying intensities; like a sudden lightning bolt or like the fluttering of a butterfly's wings.

So how do you discern what's from source energy and what's from your own subconscious, in order to take confident action? The litmus test involves three processes:

1. The thought
2. The suggested action
3. The outcome beyond the action

Focus on the outcome and pay attention to whether it feels lifeless and flat or bright and uplifting . . . and that's your answer.

The reason you focus on the outcome *beyond* the action is because the action itself often comes with apprehension attached—especially when it comes from the divine whose intention is for you to continually expand. When that's the case, your subconscious will offer up fear and self-sabotage to keep you in your comfort zone.

If, for example, you want to end an unfulfilling relationship:

1. The thought might be to resolve the relationship with respect and compassion
2. The inspired action is to have an honest, blame-free, respectful conversation with your partner to explain your intention and to work out the emotions and the practicalities around what comes next.

3.   The outcome is to move on to a happier place for both parties.

The trust part comes from keeping your focus on the outcome you want, which lies beyond the awkward conversation and the temporary discomfort of the subsequent change. If you focus on the conversation itself—which is often a stretch for anyone's level of communication skills—you're likely to avoid taking the action.

Even if you think you're ill-equipped to take the action (like in this instance, if the conversation turns into one of conflict and blame), when you're coming from a place of inspired action (inspired meaning in spirit, in connection to source energy), then regardless of the apparent immediate outcome, only good will result.

3.   **Be Courageous**
Inspired action can be a tough nut to crack. It takes courage to play a bigger game, and boldness to face your fear and do it anyway. Every time you succeed in breaking through a fear—to have a conversation, pick up the phone, e-mail a publisher, sign up for some coaching, go to the gym, give the speech, take a flight, speak up in the meeting, ask for the business or let go of control—*every time,* you'll expand as a person, grow in character and deepen your wisdom.

Step up, purposeful warrior!

Respect and Allow

"Out beyond ideas of wrongdoing and rightdoing,
there is a field. I will meet you there."

RUMI

**In this chapter you'll learn the purposefulness of you being
here now. There's a reason for your physical features, your
style of thinking, your emotional interpretations and your
soul's vision that's driving you to be, do and have more.
There's a reason for every other person's uniqueness
too—their soul has a plan and they're living out a purpose.
So how do we shift from tolerance to co-creation?**

The universe made no mistake in planning every soul that's ever
existed to come forth into physical form for a unique experience.
None is more important than another. Without you, there'd be a
hole in the jigsaw of eternity!

The expression of diversity is a glorious plan—different heights,
weights, ages, talents, beliefs, abilities, fortunes, aspirations and
life spans. Source energy intends for expansion by creating an
infinite number of unique experiences in everything through

which it pulses. Respect is allowing each person and thing to expand as its soul anticipated. The word 'respect' refers to the admiration felt towards a person or a thing, or the attention and consideration given to another.

When an individual or a society asks you to conform in a way that feels off purpose to you, it limits the spectrum of expression we are all here to have. It's logical, standing in a place of perspective, that this can lead to rebellion, conflict and separation.

In his book *Birth and Beyond*[2], Dr Yehudi Gordon defines a number of elements of family dysfunction, one of which falls under the heading of Respect for Individuality. He says of dysfunctional parents '... [*they*] are possessive and don't recognise that each of the family members has a separate identity. Often they pry into private affairs and ... there's confusion about where one person ends and where another starts. The feeling that each member of the family should behave in a certain (family) way blurs the distinction made between their individual and their collective identity.'

Freedom exists when you give yourself permission to think, feel and express yourself as you feel prompted. When what you want to be, do and have can fit into a principle of 'more for all and less for none', you can assume you're reasonably on track.

Have you heard the saying, 'You can't demand respect, you must earn it'? Respect is based on understanding. To know how another person's life plan is playing out and how it might or might not affect your own, you first have to ask some questions—sometimes lots of them!—and listen without judgement to the answers.

---

[2]   Dr Yehudi Gordon, *Birth and Beyond* ... : Vermilion, London 2002

This applies in our home lives and our work lives. Allowing others their opinion, their say and their personal expression is a fundamental human right.

When you're not clear of what you want to be, do and have, then everything and everyone will become your business, and they'll serve to distract you as you procrastinate and flounder. You watch the news, read the papers, listen to a person's opinion about someone else. These information sources are often judgemental, are frequently slanted in their viewpoint and promote the right to create a comparison of our own life against another's. The worse we can make someone else's life sound, the better we feel about ourselves—how freedom-enhancing is that?

In contrast, when you powerfully know what it is you're great at and what you're on this planet to learn, reveal and contribute, then you're going to accelerate your experience towards living in freedom every day. Freedom comes from going inside for your wisdom—developing your emotional intelligence and mastering your ability to plug soul in to source. When the student is ready, the teacher will appear. In holding the intention for growth and freedom, you'll learn techniques which remind you of your connection to all. Making small adjustments to how you think, feel and act each day will combine to change the outcome of your future. And remember, your purpose, passion and vision are unique to you.

There are certain skills worth developing to allow for personal and global self-expression, creativity and expansion.

- Respecting others as they do what looks odd or mad to you, knowing that it's part of their purpose to express themselves in that way at that time

- Allowing others (and yourself) to journey with their own style, attracting their own experiences and seeking only to understand
- Remaining in a mindset of the non-judging observer from moment to moment (I'm not going to understate how much of a skill that is to master. Like any great character trait, practice makes the difference)

Historically we've been encouraged to conform; think about generation after generation of family and work environments that limit personal growth by encouraging sameness, 'corporateness' and repetition.

Pay attention to the values you choose to live by—the education you have, the way you speak, the clothes you wear, the salary you aspire to, the car you drive, the company you keep, the expectations you hold, the holidays you take, the faith you follow, the marriage that's forever, the sports you play and your plans to retire. Ask yourself, 'How much of what I'm intending for myself has come through soul-engaged thought? How much of it is a repeat of what I've seen other people do?'

Think how challenging yet powerful it is when a new possibility is forged: the Christian woman exploring Buddhism; the son of a beef farmer choosing vegetarianism; the person wearing green to an all-black funeral; the homosexual miner in a working-class industrial community; the divorcing-and-respectful-about-it parents; the sixty-year-old couple adopting their first baby; the woman with facial burns being CEO of a top model agency; the child of drug addicts becoming a successful, international entrepreneur. These are the lives of way-showers, of game changers, of those who are exploding to express themselves, whatever their family, social or traditional constraints. It's *not* about rebellion, though—it's about each of us allowing the space for a full spectrum of expression (from ordinary to extraordinary) to thrive in ourselves and in others.

My journey is my journey; your journey is your journey; their journey is their journey. When specific paths cross, there's always a reason. You might have come up against your next opportunity to learn, and the environment and people you've attracted to you at any one time are there to facilitate this part of your growth. On the journey between where you are and where you want to be, you'll encounter many different opinions about how to 'do it right'. It's essential to practice discerning the value of this information; making up your mind about which to pay attention to going forward and which to ignore.

Your journey, your purpose, your abilities, your life experience, your style, your heritage and aspirations—these are utterly unique to you. It makes sense, then, that the subtleties of why you're making your choices are also unique, because there's so much in the mix. It's the same for other people, so be quick to listen and slow to pass opinion.

How does this step contribute to your personal and professional freedom? It frees you up from getting embroiled in other people's stuff, which in the big scheme of things is distracting *you* from your own development. Like a parachute on the back of a performance car, when you cut it free, you can drive without the resistance and just enjoy the scenery.

The Main Points

- **You are purposeful—there are no mistakes in you being you**

- **All other people in your life have a purpose in being here now**
- **Freedom is embracing your uniqueness, loving you for you**
- **Freedom is honouring other people on their journey and however they choose to contribute**
- **Further developing the skill of listening and asking questions will forge unity, respect and co-creation**

How to Take the Respect and Allow Step

1. **Stay Centred**

   Return often to the feelings that come from imagining your vision fulfilled; your perfect partnership in place, your most fulfilling career goal, or your trim body fitting into a pair of skinny jeans.

   Centredness is also referred to as 'the power of now', 'the present', or 'the peace which passes understanding'. It's gained by bringing your attention from the external to the internal, from the physical world back into the core of your being.

   - Breathe deeply for a few breaths.
   - Focus your mind on your core or solar plexus (the fist space below the centre of your rib cage).
   - Become aware of the energy that's being created there: is it excitement, happiness, expectation, anxiety, anticipation or hope?
   - Use your thoughts to shift that energy (if you can; sometimes it takes a bit of time and practice) towards peace and acceptance.

- Embrace a respect for the order of things the way they are. Allow yourself in that moment to just be.
- It's all good: there is perfect timing, perfect unfolding, and perfect journeying for each of us. Respect and allow, and trust source energy to play out the perfect plan.

2. **Keep away from Comparison**

Getting stuck, distracted, or disheartened by what other people are doing or saying isn't unusual. It creates an opportunity for us to perfect the art of allowing and, bit by bit, to separate ourselves from the good opinion of other people and to develop respect for all choices and all paths.

Comparison energetically attaches your vision to someone else's, creating drag and resistance. Respect (for yourself and for others) and allowing people to be magnificent as they are, cuts those ties and lets you step back into the flow of your own universal purpose. Just 'Bless him, bless her, bless them' as you move on with your journey.

Observation, not comparison, can be nature's way of checking that you still want what you said you want. If you slip into doubt for a time, you're going to have to revisit your original plan and either realign with it or change it to one that resonates with you again. Over time you learn to keep your own council and to check in with your centredness to get clear on the next intention you want to hold.

3. **Be Selective with Whom You Share Your Dreams**

Not everyone you spend time with has the skill set to unconditionally support you in your transformations. Some of your friends, family, or colleagues may tell you tales of caution and danger; that's their subconscious keeping *them* 'safe', as they think about *your* journey. Maybe they'll even ridicule you for thinking as big as you're daring.

Don't take their comments personally. Your life is not their life, and the best thing you can do is continue to reference back to your soul, back to the compass, back to your own vision. Send those friends love and light whenever you think about them.

The universe will send you supporters—mentors, mastermind groups, a coach, a new friend, an unexpected conversation, a family member or work colleague—and they'll be perfect for what you need.

STEP 6
Trust and Reward

"Money grows on the tree of persistence."

Japanese proverb

This step is about living in the power of now. In this chapter you'll see that taking time out of the equation accelerates results *and* creates peace of mind. Also, keeping your vision in your heart and paying attention to it influences the decisions you make every day. You are not separate from other people, from the things you want, or from source energy itself.

Trust and reward mustn't be read as 'trust *for the* reward', just in case that's what you were thinking. Trust is not a holding pattern you remain in and feel good about until you get permission to land at your destination. These two elements are subtly intertwined, and with enough of the former (trust), the latter (reward) materialises. Experiencing the reality of a reward may take a day or a year, or it may even take beyond this physical lifetime and on into future generations. The energy of trusting will undoubtedly increase the speed at which your intention is attracted into being. True mastery of trust is also a reward in itself.

The reward you want could be any number of things.

- Setting up a business making millions per year on a four-day week
- Meeting your soul mate
- Setting up and funding a trust for building schools in Romania
- Inventing affordable, sustainable, clean power sources for the planet
- Retiring while you're young enough to travel the world

Imagine you decide you want to take a ten-month road trip in your new 4x4 from the north coast of Africa to the south coast. Then, arriving in Cape Town, you're going to set up business from a coastal dream house overlooking the Indian Ocean, settling there with your family.

At the start of any journey is the thought, the intention, the vision. If you choose to use your vehicle's satellite navigation system it's going to ask for two things.

1. Confirmation of where you are right now
2. Confirmation of where you want to be

It doesn't want or need to know where you've been; that's not relevant. Neither is there relevance in packing like you packed for any previous trips. You take only what's relevant to this road trip and what you don't yet have (because you don't fully know what's going to happen), you can find, pick up and resource yourself with as you go along.

You set off. For the months you're travelling, you have priceless experiences and take on invaluable information about the

African continent—cultural differences country through country; climate adjustments; and language changes. You travel many different roads: speedy highways, monotonous pot-hole miles and satisfyingly solid, single-vehicle tracks. You travel extraordinary terrains through desert, rain forest, cities and savannah lands. You have a variety of guides: your satnav, fellow travellers and, in the most remote outback, a tribal warrior. It's all part of the adventure.

Some parts of the journey you travel much faster than expected, some you choose to spend more time on because they are unexpectedly fascinating, and some are gut-wrenchingly awful to a point where you consider taking the first flight available to any other destination in the world.

Ultimately, fourteen months later, you arrive at your sea-view home of the future. You made it! You rest for a bit. Then you think, feel, take responsibility for, take action around, respect, allow and trust your way into your next reward.

The parallels between this scenario and your real life's journey are many.

- Clarity about why you want to reach your life goals keeps you motivated on the way
- You need to know what you're starting with (character, money, experiences, contacts, the ability to learn, faith, a strong support network) and where you're heading (a self-owned company, a loving relationship, a flat tummy and healthy heart, a new peer group of friends, or a packed stadium to hear you speak)
- You don't need to have *all* the answers to get started—but you do need to get started to find the answers

- You learn lessons on the way and from many places—conversations, books, DVDs, workshops, experience, successes, challenges, observing others and asking source energy in each aware moment
- You gain wisdom from a range of people—mentors, coaches, groups, leaders, the girl in the coffee shop, your grandfather, a radio interviewee and your children
- Some years you feel like you're floating on air: 'I can't believe I've come so far and have sped through so much change in such a short time!'
- Some years are a marathon, not a sprint: 'I'll just stick to the plan, put the hours in and keep the end result in mind. Progress is happening.'
- And some years are like wading through treacle: 'Even though I know there's a reason . . . this sucks!'

Here's something worth remembering about the journey, though: *for 99 per cent of the time you're travelling, you're not at your destination—you're on the way there!*

Trust and reward is all about travelling purposefully, embracing each incredible experience. Does happiness exist only at the point you arrive? No. We'd crumble and give up if that was the case.

> *Another client, Nick, an editor-in-chief of a glossy sports magazine, said, 'The principles I learned had a massive influence on me getting my recent big promotion. In under an hour I got clear about my vision—and it was so big from where I was standing that it seemed almost too much to wish for. Defining it was incredibly liberating! Jennifer said, "Hold that intention, trust and wait." Within three months I was out of my five-year job and into a bigger one, in a new company*

on a title I loved. I work a three-day week in the office, plus a
day from home, and I made the exact figure (which was big)
that I'd named in our session. Now I've got my dream job and
a vastly improved work-life balance!'

Freedom exists in life in all the moments we acknowledge.

- I'm living on purpose
- I trust for the how
- Today I'm one step closer, one experience wiser, that much richer
- I am permanently progressing even though for months I've felt like I'm treading water
- I'm part of something so much bigger than I could conceive, and if I do nothing but breathe for the next decade, each moment will be perfect, and I'll still contribute to the expansion of all that is
- I am infinitely creative and resourceful

Dr Wayne Dyer, a present-day philosopher, author and huge influencer in the field of human transformation, said that since the beginning of recorded history, people have grown up believing six *illusions.*

- I am what I have
- I am what I do
- I am who other people think I am
- I am separate from the things I want
- I am separate from other people
- I am separate from God (or whatever your name is for the underlying power that exists in everything)

These illusions shield us from the fact that:

- You could have every luxury and opportunity on the planet, and you still wouldn't be more than you are
- You could experience the spectrum of emotions and contribute your time and talents with massive results until the day you die, and you still won't be happier than you have the opportunity to be right this second
- What other people think about you is none of your concern. They could think you were a way-shower, a no-brain, an inspiration, or a huge bore and it wouldn't change your worthiness one iota
- You are connected to all things, all experiences and all people through thought and resonance, in the same way that you have been since you were conceived
- You are connected to all people past, present and future because one force flows to and through us at all times and in all places
- Everything comes from one source—matter, space, thought, instinct, success, challenge, mountains and seas—and not only do *you* come from that source, but in your purest essence (the space and intention at the centre of your ten trillion cells), you *are* that source

The only 'I am' that is true is, 'I am that I am.' To translate, it means that you are every 'that' that you can name, think of, or observe—and that covers all that is.

Too much? Let's bring it back to some simple statements.

- Trust is your umbilical cord to the reward you want, and that reward exists in both the journey *and* the destination.

- Trust passionately, consistently and in *all* things. You can't know the distance or timings between where you are and where you want to be—and the very next inspired action or active thought you make could be your biggest breakthrough.
- Trust is closely linked to 'allowing' from the previous step. They're equally part of the skill of recognising that this moment is meant to be: it's designed precisely for you, for now. If you could stand far enough back from your life, you'd undoubtedly see that all you are, all that you contribute and all that you desire is as it should be. It's all good, and there's perfection in each moment.

The Main Points

- **Trust shifts the reward from being a destination into something that also exists in each moment**
- **There are many ways your journey can be re-routed and enriched**
- **Mastering trust reveals treasure in all encounters**
- **Pay less attention to the illusions and trust that what you want is already here**
- **However extraordinary your vision, it's perfect … and you can!**

How to Take the Trust and Reward Step

1. **Relax about Your Dream**
   Trusting requires two things.

   1. Reminding yourself of your vision and what it's going to feel like when every element is in place

2. Acknowledging that the how is for the universe to handle

Plus, just so you're prepared, that how (which is the path between where you are and where you want to be) is unlikely to take the route you think it will.

The more you can 'let go and let God', the richer will be your journey and the speedier you will reach your destination and experience your reward.

2. **Call Your Spirit Back**
    Calling your spirit back is when you notice that you've drifted into an anxiety-based 'what if', or a defensive or justifying set of thoughts. These can be prompted by something someone said to you, something you've read (that you assume must apply to you), a past experience ('Well, I didn't make money in the last venture, so why would this one be different?'), or a deeply held belief ('People like me aren't enough for a woman like that').

Or, your head might be filled with the doings of today: meetings, deadlines, spreadsheets, suppliers, clients, marketing campaigns, children, friendships, life-partner, money situation and fitness. Do you feel it?

Calling your spirit back can be a two-minute process, where you catch yourself in a moment of anxiety, reaction, anger, comparison, or judgement … and you stop.

Take a moment, take a breath and notice where your attention has gone; it'll be outside your body somewhere, at home, on a member of your team, on a project, or wherever.

Then call it back. See all of that dispersed, out-of-body energy coming back into your body and taking its rightful place inside your heart. Imagine it being recharged and polished up by the love and light that's present there. Check in with yourself how much better that feels.

While you're in this state, recall your vision—family, fitness, home, career and contribution—and give up the how to the universe before you move onward with your day.

Doing this as often as you become conscious of your energy travelling outside your body brings your creative power back under the control of your clear and courageous thinking, and of your soul itself. It's the space where trusting your infinite creativity fast-tracks the reward.

3. **Track the Breakthroughs**

This is another journaling exercise that's intended to help us be aware of the fact that we live in a friendly universe and that, in fact, all we're experiencing at any one time is contributing to the greater good.

First take a notebook, and on the first blank page draw a line down the middle. Each day, on the left side of the page write down three to five things that occurred that day which stood out for you in some way. Write them factually and without attaching judgement to them.

- 'Edward phoned and asked if he could rent the room in my flat. I said no.'
- 'Met a girl in the restaurant queue who started work last week in the tax department. We ended up having lunch together.'

- 'Swam fifty lengths this morning and lapped the guy with the silver swim cap three times.'
- 'I bought two vanilla slices at the supermarket and ate both of them when watching TV tonight.'
- 'Sally called to say her granny died.'

Over time you'll fill up the left side of each of the pages of your notebook with things that, for your own reason, stood out for you each day.

Second, designate one night per week as your journal review night. On that night, after you've written that day's standouts, look back in your journal at any eight to ten previous entries. Ask yourself this question: 'How has that event benefitted my life?'

Some of the statements will have immediate and obvious answers, which you can fill in on the right side of the page.

- 'If I'd said yes to Edward, Charlotte and I wouldn't have met, and through her I joined the spin class, which I'm loving.'
- 'I saved £445.00 on my tax return because of that loophole Eve mentioned that day at lunch. Going iPad shopping later!'
- 'Sally's a different person since not having to care for her granny. After three months, she got fit, thin and motivated; set up the company she'd be talking about for years; and has taken on her first clients. She's an inspiration!'

Some of the statements won't feel like they're ready for the 'positive take', and that's okay; eventually, in their own right time, they'll fully play out. In time, what you'll create is a personal record of how apparently random events, decisions and other people's place in your life have contributed over time to a pattern of learning, growth and confirmation of the friendliness of the universe.

It underpins the skill of trust and will confirm that all things in the moment have their reward.

STEP 7
Enduring Gratitude

"Develop an attitude of gratitude, and give thanks for everything that happens to you, knowing that every step forward is a step toward achieving something bigger and better than your current situation."

Brian Tracy

This final step is far from ethereal; it's practical and takes discipline. In this chapter you'll cover what sorts of thoughts create what sort of results.

Energy follows attention. When you pay attention to the highest vibrating thoughts we know of—joy, knowledge, empowerment, freedom, love and gratitude—you're creating with the most powerful and leveraged energy available to you.

There are two types of gratitude. The first is a light gratitude—a kind of partial software version, if you like. This is the gratitude that most of us use for being thankful for what we observe about and around ourselves. For example, you're grateful for your home, food on the table, your friends and family, your children being healthy, your job, a great holiday this year … you get the picture?

Light gratitude can also be subtly used as positive but remains very close to tipping into a lower vibration if you're not paying close enough attention. You've heard the style, like when someone says, 'Well, it's better than having to walk *all* the way home,' or 'At least I only had one month I couldn't pay off my credit card.'

Do you feel it? It positions the situation as something better and whilst it's a great start in practicing the skill set of gratitude, and will get you results over time, there is a more powerful type of gratitude available to you.

Enduring gratitude is a way of being. It's a mindset worth developing because it shifts your life experience from 'I' to 'all', from separation to unity, and from limitation to freedom.

If you didn't already know it, there's a four-stage process which we go through in everything we learn.

1. **Unconscious Incompetence**: We don't yet know that we don't know. Take learning to drive, for example. At fourteen you don't even realise that driving is something you're going to need to learn when the 'parent taxi' comes to a halt!
2. **Conscious Incompetence:** We have awareness that a new skill set is going to benefit our lives, so we set out to learn it and practice it. You start your driving lessons and realise it's actually really tough to coordinate pedals, gear sticks, mirrors and road rules. You can't

imagine how every other road user seems to manage so effortlessly and it's an uncomfortable place to be.

3. **Conscious Competence:** Over time we practice the skill set and it becomes easier for us to use it day-to-day. With practice, your driving becomes more skilled and manageable. You don't have to tell yourself, 'Mirror, signal, manoeuvre.' You begin to just do it and your confidence grows.

4. **Unconscious Competence:** We've practiced to such a level that we're no longer aware we ever couldn't do it; it's become part of our repertoire of life skills along with millions of other things. Your driving is effortless and mainly instinctive. Pedals, lights, gears, breaking, parking—you're a natural!

Developing enduring gratitude takes this learning process and more; it engages the physical, intellectual, emotional and spiritual parts of yourself, achieving a result that borders on rapture. It's like a shift from generally fit to world-class athlete. It requires all four human elements to engage in the process.

If we take a fitness example, say you want to achieve muscle tone, lose weight and increase self-esteem. You know it's something you have to form a habit around, so you've established a *desire*.

Then there's the *decision* about how to get the desired results. You decide the method will be to swim fifty lengths a day, followed by fifty sit-ups, with the intention of increasing them to one hundred each over the next several months.

The *action* you then take is fuelled by the desire and the decision—the feelings and thoughts about the process and the end result are already in place—that's what get's you out to the pool every day.

In a very short space of time, you'll notice the *evidence*: your increased energy, reduced waistline and growing confidence. These in turn provide ongoing *motivation,* which prompts you to *repeat* the actions.

As time passes, your hundred lengths followed by hundred sit-ups just becomes 'what I do' as a matter of course. At this point you're in *mastery.* This is the process you're looking to achieve with your attitude of gratitude. Mastery of the skill will come in time with practice, patience and persistence.

Applying those stages to master enduring gratitude could look like the following.

- **Desire**—you want to always live in freedom—body, mind, heart and soul—personally and professionally
- **Decision**—you'll be grateful for everything, at all times, regardless of whether it appears positive or negative in the moment
- **Action**—you will pay attention to your thoughts and reframe any that aren't in gratitude with thoughts that are
- **Evidence**—your raised resonance will attract to you a new set of circumstances, conversations, friends, experiences and opportunities
- **Motivation**—you use the excitement from the evidence to fire you up
- **Repetition**—you keep doing what's working and make revisions where something could be working better

- **Mastery**—without knowing it, one day you simply *are* enduring gratitude; you are unconsciously competent

If the universe is friendly, if its core characteristic is love, then it is grateful for every expression of itself whether in physical or non-physical form. This is without exception. If source energy is grateful for and in all things, and that resonance is the default of every cell of your body, your alignment with enduring gratitude will give you freedom the likes of which you've never known.

T.S. Eliot said it like this, "We shall not cease from exploration. And the end of all our exploring will be to arrive where we started … and know the place for the first time."

As you learn this enduring gratitude step, as with all the others, your soul's knowing of it's connection to source energy will inspire you to keep going and to trust the process.

> *Cerriden, a successful London therapist, said, 'In the past six weeks, since implementing the Seven Steps, I have had the unusual experience of people giving me things and paying for things for me—a wonderful break in a hugely expensive and beautiful hideaway, an offer of house sitting, a gift of five visits to a spa, a meal at the Gherkin. It's bizarre!*

> *'Every time I park in a pay car park, someone drives by and gives me their ticket that still has plenty of time on it! I've had offers of help on a project I've been trying to get under way for some time. Several times I have taken stuff to be fixed—small things, but they still usually cost money—and when I ask how much I owe, the person says, "Oh, that's okay, don't worry about it!"*

Am I going round in clothes full of holes, looking downtrodden? Quite the reverse: I'm tanned and full of energy. I seem to be in a happy bubble despite the alarming progress of the recession and my proximity to the current London riots.'

The Main Points

- **Enduring gratitude is the most powerfully leveraging energy you can work with**
- **Light gratitude is** *doing***; enduring gratitude is** *being***—both have value**
- **As you practice, keep in mind the four-stage learning process**
- **Intend with desire, decisiveness, action, evidence, motivation and repetition until you reach mastery**
- **Expect source energy to keep you encouraged and inspired; ultimately, your success is creation's success**

How to Take the Enduring Gratitude Step

1. Practice Reframing

Reframing is a method of thought adjustment to look at an experience in a way that serves you more favourably: same picture, different context, richer overall experience.

For example, say you're passed over for a promotion you've applied for at work. The first set of thoughts might be, 'I can't believe I didn't get that. My boss has always had it in for me; she's always liked that new guy better. I'll never make the next level; I'm such a loser.'

A reframe in that situation would be, 'I'm glad I put my name in for that promotion. I'm grateful the company is aware I want to progress. I didn't get this position this time, so I'll get the feedback and commit to learning whatever it is that would have made the difference. In the meantime I'm going to get my CV up to date and hold an intention that the right position, in the right team and in the right company will come up for me. My vision remains clear and courageous. I trust the universe is purposefulness in all things and I'm grateful.'

Do you sense the shift in energy? It's a series of thoughts over which you are ultimately in control. You can adjust them in the moment or when you're reviewing a situation. The new thought, with higher energy, creates a neural pathway in your brain. The more often you reframe towards increased gratefulness, the deeper those neural pathways become and the more easily you can reframe all future instances.

Reframing is a never-ending upward cycle of gratefulness resulting in off-the-scale opportunities, fulfilment and freedom.

2. **The '... or Better' Strategy**
   When you define what it is that you want to aspire to next, sometimes you're simply not able to conceive how 'blown-away amazing' a solution that the universe (source energy) can come up with for you.

   The '... or better' strategy is one where after you've stated or thought your expectation, you simple add '... or better' to the end of it. It could be, 'My sea-view barn conversion is a stunning and safe place for me and my family to live. We're inspired in this home, spend quality time together, and my home office is an ideal place for my clients to come to and be motivated for higher results ... *or better.'*

No matter how great you can create—you can't out-create the creator! If you put the law of gratitude on a numeric scale and use the first principle that *thoughts become things*, your unaware thoughts to date may already be attracting 20 per cent of the total abundance available to you into your life.

Getting clear and courageous, over a short time, could allow you to more than double that abundance to, say, 50 per cent of the total possible abundance. That's amazing for you, because it's already so much bigger than you ever could have imagined from the lifetime of experiences you've accrued to date.

However, by developing gratitude on a day-to-day basis, *and* adding '... or better' to your vision or to your statements of intention, it energetically creates space for the universe to consistently get creative and do its thing on your behalf. Every time the universe over-delivers, adding icing to your already rich cake in return for adding two little words, you'll increase your ability to trust and begin to expect the unexpected '... or better'!

3. **Daily Gratitude**
    Write or recall five things at the end of every day that you're grateful for. It's a powerfully simple exercise with simply powerful results.

The Seven Steps to Personal and Professional Freedom
How to Add Meaning to Your Ambition

Your 'How to' Steps

STEP 1: Clear and Courageous Thinking

1. Get clear on your vision and write it down
2. Create a vision board
3. Commit to a five-minute focus, morning and night

Step 2: Feel It to Reveal It—Attracting Your Vision

1. Pay attention to your emotional shifts
2. Consciously choose better feeling thoughts
3. Choose a one-step dial up in vibration

Step 3: Absolute Personal Responsibility

1. Give up blaming
2. Be accountable

Step 4: Take Inspired Action

1. Learn to interpret your intuition
2. Focus beyond the action to the outcome
3. Be courageous—do the thing you fear

Step 5: Respect and Allow

1. Stay centred and re-reference inside for your highest purpose
2. Keep away from comparison
3. Be selective with whom you share your dreams

Step 6: Trust and Reward

1. Relax about your dream
2. Call your spirit back
3. Track your breakthroughs

Step 7: Enduring Gratitude

1. Practice reframing all situations to find a resonance that uplifts you
2. Add '… or better' to each thought and vision
3. Daily gratitude—write down five things